Ridgeland Revealed

Guide to the Architecture of the

Ridgeland-Oak Park Historic District

•

Oak Park Historic Preservation Commission

Edited by Arlene Sanderson

Village of Oak Park, Oak Park, Illinois

1993

International Standard Book Number: 0-9616915-1-4
Library of Congress Cataloging-in-Publication Data
Ridgeland revealed: guide to the Ridgeland Oak Park Historic District/Oak Park
Historic Preservation Commission; edited by Arlene Sanderson.

p.   cm.

Includes bibliographical references and index.
ISBN 0-9616915-1-4

1. Historic buildings—Illinois—Ridgeland—Guidebooks. 2. Architecture—
Illinois—Ridgeland—Guidebooks. 3. Ridgeland (Ill.)—Buildings, structures, etc.—
Guidebooks. I. Sanderson, Arlene, 1953-   . II. Oak Park Historic
Preservation Commission.

F549.R48R53   1993   93-639
917.73'64—dc20

The Village of Oak Park, Oak Park, Illinois 60302
© 1993 by the Village of Oak Park, a municipal corporation.
Printed in the United States of America

Designed by Sherry L. Miller
Cover photograph of John Farson house by Erik S. Lieber

Table of Contents

How to Use This Guide

This guidebook serves as both a tour manual and reference. The introductory essay establishes a historical context for the towns of Ridgeland and Oak Park and describes the evolution of residential, ecclesiastical and commercial architecture within the historic district. References to specific sites are listed in brackets.

The core of the book is devoted to 79 sites. A description of each site's characteristic or distinct architectural features is presented along with a photograph. The architect, date and original client are identified when known.

Each site is numbered and referenced on a map that appears on the inside back cover. The key opposite the map includes site numbers and addresses for ease in consulting the text.

In a few instances, architecturally or historically significant buildings in close proximity but outside the official boundaries of the Ridgeland-Oak Park Historic District were included. Biographical information on local architects and a bibliography are provided for further reference.

Please note: *The majority of buildings in this book are privately owned and residential. Please respect the owner's privacy and remain on the sidewalk or public areas. Pleasant Home, 217 S. Home Ave., and Unity Temple, 875 Lake St., are open for regularly scheduled guided tours. Contact the Oak Park Visitors Center (708) 848-1500 for tour information.*

The streets and neighborhoods of the Ridgeland-Oak
Park Historic District provide a fascinating visual record
of the transformation of small towns into suburban
America and the evolution of residential architectural
styles after the mid nineteenth century.

As railroads advanced westward beyond the city
of Chicago, the founding fathers of Ridgeland and
Oak Park conceived the adjoining towns as residential
communities inhabited by commuters. The villages
attracted potential buyers accustomed to the amenities
of urban life, yet seeking the quiet and freedom
beyond the city. Ridgeland and Oak Park grew and
prospered side by side. In 1902 they consolidated
and incorporated as the Village of Oak Park.

Unique to the Ridgeland-Oak Park Historic District
are intact historic neighborhoods documenting the
changing popularity of various architectural styles
between 1852 and 1940. Succeeding waves of
construction changed the appearance of single-family
homes from eclectic Victorian to turn-of-the-century,
stucco styles or the simple, geometric designs of Frank
Lloyd Wright and the Prairie style architects living
and working in Oak Park.

The district's architectural diversity also documents
the impact of social change on residential design.
As the demand for housing grew, the village was one
of the first communities to rise to the challenge
of apartment house construction and pioneered the
development of comprehensive zoning.

Remarkably few of the smaller, earlier homes
were demolished to accommodate the construction
of multi-family residences. Larger complexes were
restricted to locations along main or peripheral streets
like Austin and Ridgeland avenues or Washington
and South boulevards where collectively they envelop

neighborhoods of single-family, older houses. Numerous apartment buildings were designed with features generally reserved for individual residences and have courtyards that introduce landscaping and reduce the mass of the street facade.

By 1910, most of the major religious and civic structures in the district were built. Churches dominate the corner lots of many blocks where their scale and stylistic variety complement the surrounding architecture. Early commercial structures were built in close proximity to commuter train depots that continue to serve as the focus of local business districts.

By 1940, the historic district was largely built as it stands today. The adoption of a comprehensive plan for the Village of Oak Park in 1973 furthered a growing awareness of the distinctions between adjoining neighborhoods and inspired the establishment of the Ridgeland-Oak Park Historic District.

In 1983 the Ridgeland district became the second area within the village to earn a listing on the National Register of Historic Places. Ten years earlier, the Frank Lloyd Wright Prairie School of Architecture Historic District had been established.

The Oak Park Historic Preservation Commission has published this guide to promote an understanding and appreciation among local residents and visitors of the architectural diversity and neighborhood integrity preserved within the Ridgeland-Oak Park Historic District.

David Sokol
Oak Park, Illinois

Acknowledgements

The Oak Park Historic Preservation Commission authorized a committee of volunteers to develop this guide to the architecture of the Ridgeland-Oak Park Historic District. Numerous individuals have lent their time, expertise and talents to this task.

Daniel M. Bluestone, Columbia University professor of architectural history, played an instrumental role in gaining National Register status for the district. The introductory essay in this guidebook is based on his nominating report. David Sokol, professor and chair of the history of architecture and art department at the University of Illinois at Chicago, contributed the foreword.

Stephen J. Kelley, commissioner, architect and engineer, researched and wrote the section on local churches. Leslie Gilmore, commissioner and architect, wrote the section on commercial structures. Michael Culhane completed the initial survey of records and sites, and prepared the profiles on local architects.

The responsibility of researching and writing individual building entries was shared by: Judith Rood, historian, Elizabeth Scanlan, commissioner and architect, Deborah Slaton, architect and historian, and Peg Zak, commissioner and community historian. Judith Hull and Joseph Hoerner also worked on this project. The role of committee chair was assumed by Judah Graubart and then by Elizabeth Scanlan.

The support and encouragement of commission chairpersons Frank Heitzman, Margaret Klinkow, John Mojonnier and David Sokol, as well as that of all present and former commissioners who shared their appreciation and knowledge of specific buildings, is gratefully acknowledged.

The Frank Lloyd Wright Home and Studio Foundation's tour center and bookshop staff consulted on the design, use and marketing of the book. The Foundation's research center was an important source of reference material, as were the files of the Historical Society of Oak Park and River Forest. The committee is particularly grateful to Carol Kelm, executive director of the historical society, and Bill Jerousek, local history librarian at the Oak Park Public Library, for their assistance.

Gary Holm-Bertelsen, Erik Lieber and Leslie Schwartz took the contemporary photographs for the guidebook. These images are on permanent loan to the historical society, which provided the historic photographs. The committee also wishes to thank Fred Zinke, senior planner for the Village of Oak Park, and the clerical staff of Village Hall.

This guide contains only a sample of the many notable structures in the historic district. Sites were selected for inclusion on the basis of their historical significance, architectural and stylistic integrity, originality, or association with an important architect.

The authors are indebted to the Oak Park residents and building owners whose research, responses and anecdotal accounts about structures in the Ridgeland-Oak Park Historic District provided information when records were nonexistent. Finally, we wish to acknowledge the owners and caretakers who have preserved and restored the work of Oak Park's first residents, and who "by purpose and perseverance ... have built up a beautiful town."

Historical Context

The Ridgeland-Oak Park Historic District is an L-shaped, 1½-square-mile section of residential and commercial property in the heart of Oak Park. The borders extend from Lake Street and Chicago Avenue south to Madison Avenue and from Austin Boulevard west to Harlem Avenue. The district's boundaries cross lines once defining the neighboring towns of Ridgeland and Oak Park.

In 1898, when several western municipalities were debating whether to remain independent or merge with the city of Chicago, residents of Ridgeland and Oak Park voted to remain autonomous. The towns merged and incorporated in 1902 as the Village of Oak Park.

The settlement and growth of the suburb paralleled the social changes and expansion in many midwestern cities in the mid to late 1800s. The appeal of open spaces, clean air, affordable land and the prospect of owning a single-family home inspired the adventurous to seek the quiet and freedom of the borderland.

Small towns grew alongside the railroads that found ready markets among consumers and commuters requiring convenient and regular access to the city. Many of the 90,000 people left homeless in the disastrous 1871 Chicago fire fled to the developing suburbs. The towns of Ridgeland and Oak Park, just eight miles west of the city, were prime territory for development and settlement.

Early Settlers and Developers

In 1837 Joseph Kettlestrings, the founder of Oak Park, purchased a 172-acre tract in western Cook County for $216. In 1849, the Chicago and Galena Union Railroad established a passenger stop called Harlem a few blocks west of its present location. Kettlestrings began to subdivide his holdings in 1856. As sections of the land were sold and developed, Kettlestrings Grove was renamed Oak Ridge and finally Oak Park in 1871.

In 1863 enterprising real estate investors James W. Scoville and Milton Niles followed Kettlestrings lead and subdivided forty acres of land south of Lake Street and the railroad tracks. Construction began along Maple Street, launching the first major settlement in what is now the historic district.

After the Chicago fire and the establishment in 1872 of a

railroad depot within the borders of Oak Park, the village's population surged. In ten years the number of residents grew from an estimated 500 to 2,000; by 1900 the population reached almost 10,000.

Ridgeland

Scoville continued to expand his real-estate holdings. He pooled his resources with William B. Ogden, Joel D. Harvey and Josiah Lombard to purchase a larger tract of land. For $700 an acre, they acquired the territory north of the tracks to Chicago Avenue and east of Oak Park Avenue to Austin Boulevard. This parcel was subdivided in 1872 and became the basis for the historic town of Ridgeland.

Scoville earned a fortune in real estate and became an important civic leader and philanthropist. He is generally credited with planting trees and constructing the streets, sidewalks and sewers that made the area attractive to potential buyers. In the 1880s, records of the Ridgeland Improvement Association stated, "Houses are in good demand. There has not been a vacant house in months."

The Ridgeland train stop was simply a signal flag at first. However, a four-room depot was soon built with funds solicited from

James W. Scoville (1825-1893)

local property owners. A small commercial district developed at the intersection of Lake Street and Ridgeland Avenue.

Until 1879 when the first Ridgeland school was constructed, children attended school in the back room of F. Dore's store at Lake Street and Ridgeland Avenue. Older students walked to Central School in Oak Park.

By 1888, Ridgeland was in the process of building and equipping its own firehouse as well as a community hall. Both were two-story brick structures on Lake Street. The town hall had two shops on the ground floor, while the second floor was a meeting space complete with a stage. Ridgeland was generally remembered for its active social rather than political life.

The Standard of Civilization

Oak Park and Ridgeland developed simultaneously, sharing many of the same challenges and resources. High ground favored settlement, but the proximity of the Des Plaines River and seasonal rains assured regular flooding. Local histories describe the territory of Ridgeland in the spring as "a good-sized lake." During winter people could skate all the way into the city on the ice rink formed when submerged land froze.

For several decades, planners debated the design of a system of ditches and closed sewers. Construction finally began in the mid 1880s. In 1888, an agreement with the newly organized Cicero Water, Gas and Electric Light Company assured residents "pure, wholesome water" pumped from nine artesian wells at Lake Street and Oak Park Avenue.

Lake Street, the main thoroughfare crossing Ridgeland and Oak Park, was maintained by Henry W. Austin and Scoville as a toll road until 1878. Travelers could view the impressive mansions lining both sides of the street. Those wishing to avoid the tariff could negotiate a trail that later developed into Madison Street or the Chicago Avenue "cow path." Farther north was Augusta Boulevard, otherwise known as "the big ditch."

In 1878 only six trains traveled daily between Oak Park and the city. Service increased with demand, and by 1885 there were thirty daily trains; by 1894 there were eighty.

Two waiting rooms flanked the central entrance and ticket booth at the first Ridgeland train depot.

The Chicago, Harlem and Batavia rail line, which terminated at the Forest Park cemeteries, began operating in 1882. Termed a "dummy line" because its small locomotives were disguised with wooden side panels to deceive skittish horses, this short-lived rail service earned a reputation for being undependable. The dummy line tracks ran along Randolph Street in an area now reserved for parkways. By 1891, a network of streetcars and electrical trains helped meet the demand for reliable, inexpensive transporation.

As in Ridgeland in the 1880s, Oak Park patrons demanded and paid for a train station at Oak Park Avenue, an important step in the commercial development of the historic district. Shops, banks and related businesses clustered around rail stops at Ridgeland, Oak Park, Marion and Harlem establishing the retail and commercial centers of village life today.

Shops and businesses lined both sides of Oak Park Avenue north of the train tracks by 1903.

In 1888, the Scoville Institute, named for its chief benefactor, opened at the corner of Lake Street and Grove Avenue. The structure housed a lending library, community center and gymnasium. Seven public schools and at least 15 churches served the local community by the turn of the century.

William Halley, the author of *Pictorial Oak Park* in 1898

expressed the hometown pride and aspirations of early residents:

> Our only claim is that by purpose and perseverance we have built up a beautiful town that is possessed of every home advantage. We have reclaimed the wilderness, have set up the standard of civilization and now freely offer of what we have to those who appreciate our labors and are desirous of joining us in the good work of making life more enjoyable, time more precious and results more certain.

● **Residential Architecture**

Early Houses: Vernacular and Italianate

The Garland house, which was moved to 241 S. Home Ave., is believed to be the oldest surviving house in the district (ca. 1852) [9]. According to Gertrude Hoagland's *Historical Survey of Oak Park, Illinois,* the first four houses actually built in the district were constructed in 1867 on Maple Avenue. Other early dwellings that survive date from the 1870s and 1880s. As public records of these dates are not available, owners, architects or builders are rarely known.

The district's older houses are usually Gothic or Italianate. Both styles are characterized by tall, narrow window openings with elaborate trim caps at the head of the windows. The Gothic cottages have steeply pitched roofs and fretwork at the gable ends. Low roofs, bracketed eaves, window bays, and rectangular or asymmetrical plans are stylistic features of the Italianate designs [1, 17, 67].

Victorian Residences and Individuality (1880-1900)

The historic district's major Victorian residences, built in the later decades of the nineteenth century, were designed largely in the Stick and Queen Anne styles. The irregular shapes of gables, dormers, eaves, bay windows and porches were asymmetrically disposed and introduced picturesque variety [3, 7, 15, 22, 23, 36].

The designs seem to strive for individual expression, craftsmanship, and distinction. The district includes several fine examples of Queen Anne houses by architects Normand S. Patton, Henry G. Fiddelke and Wesley A. Arnold [7, 20, 24, 25]. Rowhouse developments revealed the same striving for individual distinction [18].

Contemporary concerns for sunlight and health popularized open porches, bay windows, and the interpenetration of interior and exterior spaces. The dominant roof, picturesque chimneys and interlocking masses symbolized domestic intimacy and family life to the middle-class Chicagoans moving to Oak Park and Ridgeland. The complex exterior surfaces mirrored the compartmentalized interiors with inglenooks, window bays, sunrooms and porches.

Typical Victorian interiors were richly decorated with patterned rugs, wallcoverings and upholstery, as well as ornately carved furniture.

William J. Van Keuren built dozens of elaborate Stick and Queen Anne style houses in the district, as well as scaled-down versions of the same design for clients with more limited budgets [3]. This practice was common among builders, too. R. G. Hancock, Frederick A. Hill, J. Kempston and Son, and A. D. Orvis produced streetscapes where modest houses relate to grander designs [46, 66].

In the early years of this century, the popularity of picturesque designs waned as Oak Park architects and builders developed quieter, simpler, more symmetrical and formal houses. The concern for a community of forms replaced earlier assertions of individuality [19, 25, 33, 61].

Simplicity and Repose in the Modern Home (1897-1920)

George W. Maher's 1897 design of a house for John Farson, 217 S. Home Ave., anticipated the new direction of the district's domestic architecture [8]. Following the Farson construction, detached residences in the district increasingly adopted the simplicity and quiet repose of Maher's design. Projecting dormers, towers, bays and porches were restrained or eliminated, leaving a simplified, rectangular, "minimal" house.

A combination of aesthetic, social and cultural developments influenced this transformation in residential architecture. The classical building styles adopted and popularized by the 1893 World's Columbian Exposition found an appreciative audience among mainstream architects and members of the general public who interpreted the designs as suggesting unity and harmony in a chaotic urban world.

The economic depression of the 1890s engendered criticism of the excesses of sham historical ornament, and fostered a desire to modernize and simplify home decoration. Tenement house crusades and housing reform generally led architects to seek models of simple, inexpensive homes.

Plain wall surfaces, natural wood trim, built-in cabinetry and geometric art glass designs combined to create the simple, linear styling of Prairie style interiors.

In addition, a nascent public health movement and theories about the transmission of disease raised fears that the nooks, bays, uneven surfaces and irregular plans of Victorian houses might harbor dirt, dust and dangers. New household technology and efforts to reform women's work emphasized comfort, convenience and simplicity.

Interest in the Arts and Crafts movement fostered an aesthetic of sparseness favoring plain, natural surfaces rather than complex, decorative designs. Many of these influences coalesced dramatically in the work of Frank Lloyd Wright and other contemporary Prairie style architects, such as Maher, John S. Van Bergen and Eben Ezra Roberts, working in Oak Park [12, 13, 26, 34, 43, 49, 51].

Wright introduced stucco to the streets of Oak Park. The medium was perfectly suited to the radical geometric abstraction and plain surfaces of his Prairie style designs. Roberts, too, was a strong proponent of stucco. His lengthy career and widespread local popularity created a market for the medium, which explains the prevalence of stucco houses in the district.

The introduction of modern stucco residential architecture and its striking continuity from one house to the next gave the district's streetscapes a new unity. Stylistic unity is also evident in the rows of frame and stucco residences on North Taylor, the 200 block of Pleasant Avenue, South Elmwood and South Harvey, where between 1900 and 1920, builders popularized the lessons and forms of Maher, Roberts and other Prairie style architects [66].

Frederick A. Hill, a contractor and builder, was responsible for constructing hundreds of houses in the eastern section of the district using plans by Frederick Schock, Van Keuren and other architects. Hill also directed his attention to a unified streetscape. He planted countless trees along the parkways. In 1914 he attempted to develop gateways with monumental urns where Harlem and Austin avenues intersect Washington Boulevard.

Elsewhere in the district, R. G. Hancock constructed entire blocks of uniform California bungalows. According to a March 18, 1916, article in the *Oak Leaves*, "The general style of the building lends an air of refinement and exclusiveness not possible where the types of building vary greatly and no defined building restrictions are followed" [38, 56]. In the early years of this century, the local press was a strong advocate of "building restrictions."

"Impending Calamity": Apartment and the Suburb

Oak Park's proximity to Chicago and accessible transportation made it a desirable place to live. Apartment buildings were a logical solution to accommodating the large numbers of people who wished to enjoy these advantages. Oak Park homeowners, however, began to view the modern apartment building with growing alarm as a threat to their unified streetscape, to their ideal of "a community of homes" and to their property values.

Few building issues, if any, were as controversial as the proper place of apartment buildings within the village. Irony pervaded the debate. The same forces advocating the reform of domestic life and the design of a simple, more efficient detached residence also fostered the turn toward apartment living. Apartments offered comfort and convenience without the responsibility and cost of homeownership.

The district's significance as a model of community planning centers upon the village's fairly successful resolution of the social and design challenges raised by the apartment building in the suburb. An editorial in the April 22, 1905, issue of the *Oak Leaves* entitled "The Impending Calamity" aptly and pointedly expressed the widespread resistance to the apartment building.

> Oak Park is threatened with an invasion— a foreign invasion— of flats. The advance guard of the enemy is already upon us and the great host of its army is encamped at our very borders. ... Oak Park has stood thus far for that distinctive type of individual and community life that has its dependence upon broad expanse of open space, upon grass and trees and sunlight and fresh air. When it ceases to stand for that, it ceases to be Oak Park.

On May 27, the editor attacked standard apartment building design as a threat to public health. Usurping the open spaces devoted to lawns and trees around detached residences, "The flat destroys all this and gives in its place a lot of dry-goods, box architecture lined up on the street without beauty and forming a bar to the circulation of fresh air and the accessibility of sunshine, nature's two great health-givers."

The furor over apartment buildings led to calls for social restraint on the part of landowners, and for ordinances and regulation on the part of the local government. A 1902 ordinance required apartment buildings housing three or more families to be constructed of brick, stone, iron or other noncombustible material. The ordinance required fire escapes and dictated how much of the lot the building could cover. Building heights were limited to half the width of the broadest adjacent street (roughly thirty-three to forty feet). Minimums were established for the dimensions of light courts, rooms and windows, as well as the number of sinks and toilets in each unit.

The small, two-flat apartment building proved to be the least objectionable to residents of Oak Park. Roberts earned particular praise from contemporary writers for developing a two-flat building that blended harmoniously with single-family residences. His designs succeeded in disguising their multi-family character by following the same basic site plan and building outline as the single-family house and obscuring or tucking away the second entry [41, 42].

While the building ordinance did not ban larger apartment buildings, general resistance did affect their design. In 1907, even the local newspaper conceded that Roberts' design for Luther Conant's "Quadrangle" apartments was an exception to the "impending calamity," a building in harmony with community ideals [40].

Although few of the apartments built between 1905 and 1920 in the district achieved the site and architectural character of the Quadrangle, many similar elements were integrated in other designs. Architects and builders made obvious attempts to incorporate features usually reserved for the construction of single-family houses: tile roofs, casement windows, art glass and a variety of exterior ornament. Landscaped courtyards, porches and sunrooms divided the facade into less-imposing, related forms and served to link the design of multi-family structures to individual homes [6, 21, 29, 31, 50, 52, 53, 55, 58, 62, 69].

● **Church Architecture**

Religious services began in Oak Park in the 1850s in a two-room, wood-frame building known as the "little white school" at the northwest corner of Lake Street and Forest Avenue. Built in 1855, this building was donated by Joseph Kettlestrings and Henry Austin for use as a school and meeting house.

The modest structure earned the title "the mother of churches," because it housed so many congregations before their own church buildings were constructed. The site also became the home of Temperance Hall, the headquarters of the local temperance movement.

One block away, Presbyterians and Episcopalians held services above a store in Elisha Hoard's building at Lake and Marion streets. The second floor of the 1876 building was a public hall where Oak Parkers "danced during the week and prayed on Sunday."

The 1870s and '80s witnessed the construction of many churches in the district. The Unitarians and Universalists met at Temperance Hall until 1872 when they built a church at Wisconsin Avenue near Pleasant Street. Fire destroyed this structure, and they commissioned Frank Lloyd Wright to design a new church on a narrow corner lot at Lake Street and Kenilworth Avenue.

Across the street in 1873, the Congregationalists had constructed a large, stone edifice known as First Church. In 1889, members of the Second (now Pilgrim) Congregational Church moved into a a newly completed chapel at 460 Lake St. Prior to that time they had been holding services in the local train depot.

The congregation of the Euclid Avenue Methodist Church met in a single-story structure from 1899 to 1906 when the second story was completed.

The Methodists dedicated the brick First Methodist Church on the northeast corner of Lake Street and Forest Avenue in 1873.

In 1899, the Euclid Avenue Methodist congregation moved into a chapel designed by Wesley A. Arnold. The red sandstone church served the congregation until 1922 when the current stone structure was built.

The Episcopalians built their first church on Forest Avenue north of Ontario Street in 1883 and later Grace Church at 924 Lake St. The Baptists erected a brick church on the southeast corner of Wisconsin Avenue and Pleasant Street in 1883. The congregation moved to a new structure on Ontario Street in 1923.

After 1886, the Presbyterians attended church in a wood-frame building on the south side of Lake Street and in 1901 constructed a substantial stone building on the same site. Before 1864, the First Evangelical Church conducted services for Lutherans in German at Temperance Hall. The Oak Park Lutheran Church at Oak Park Avenue and Van Buren Street offered services in English in 1911. Members of this congregation went on to establish Good Shepherd Lutheran Church, 611 Randolph St., in 1941.

Community intolerance of the time denied Oak Park's Catholic residents an official place of worship. They were unable to rent a suitable space and had to meet in an abandoned barn on the Scoville estate or travel to St. Luke's Church in River Forest. John Farson, a wealthy and prominent Oak Parker, intervened and helped quell resistance to a local parish. St. Edmund was established in 1907 [27].

The tall spires of many of these structures, particularly those of First Baptist, First Methodist, Unity and First Church, served as visible landmarks for the surrounding area and earned Oak Park the nickname "Saints' Rest." These same four churches were destroyed by fire. The tall steeples of First Church and Unity Church became lightning rods setting fire to the attached buildings. As a result, later churches featured shorter and more substantially massed stone towers. Pilgrim Congregational is the district's only surviving 19th-century church.

Less obvious but of no less significance in the later design of local churches was their predominantly fireproof construction. The reconstruction of First Church in 1917 utilized steel and concrete in a manner that, according to the church herald, was "practically fireproof" and set a standard for 20th-century village churches [75]. First Methodist and First Baptist Church used similar construction techniques.

Frank Lloyd Wright's Unity Temple is widely recognized as an early example of the use of reinforced concrete as both a structural and architectural material. Here, too, the congregation's concern with fire protection influenced the choice of building material [76].

The district's churches provide a fascinating record of construction procedures. The local Presbyterian congregation took out a loan to build their 1901 church, which is now Calvary Memorial [79]. The building was completed in one construction season, but the loan took many years to repay.

Grace Episcopal Church existed as a 12-foot high structure with a flat roof until funds were raised and the sanctuary completed in 1905. The bell tower was not completed until 1922 [78].

Pilgrim Congregational's south wing chapel was erected in 1889. After a ten-year lapse, the building program continued with expanded plans that retained the style of the original building [70].

Euclid Avenue Methodist Church existed for seven years as a single story, flat-roofed edifice. The second story was added in 1906, but soon proved too small to house the growing congregation. Plans to double the size of the church foundered with the outbreak of World War I. In 1921, the building campaign was revived, and the earlier structure was replaced with the present Gothic style church [32].

The district's churches represent a wide and eclectic array of building styles. The 1893 World's Columbian Exposition fostered an interest in classical architecture that was matched with an enthusiasm for the medieval in church design. Church architects of this period studied historic structures in detail and selected components from one or several styles to incorporate into their own designs. Conscious attempts were made to imitate Romanesque and Gothic buildings in the design of many local churches.

The varied architectural styles of district churches include: the English Gothic First Church, the French Gothic St. Catherine of Siena and St. Edmund School, the Richardsonian Romanesque First Presbyterian Church, and the Shingle style of Pilgrim Congregational Church.

As a group the churches of Oak Park stand in sharp contrast to Frank Lloyd Wright's Unity Temple, a building design without traditional historical precedent.

● Commercial Buildings

The Ridgeland-Oak Park Historic District includes major retail and business areas located along Lake Street, on Oak Park Avenue south of Lake Street, at Ridgeland Avenue and Lake Street, as well as small clusters of commercial buildings at major intersections.

The first commercial enterprises in Oak Park were located on Lake Street between Harlem Avenue and Marion Street. Here, sometime after 1835, Joseph Kettlestrings opened a tavern. By 1860 a cobbler, harnessmaker, physician, druggist, building supplier and general store owner were operating places of business. A list of firms published in 1885 establishes a four- or five-block section of Lake Street west of Marion Street as the main commercial thoroughfare.

In 1876 Elisha Hoard constructed a brick building at the southwest corner of Lake and Marion streets. The first floor of "Hoard's Block" was devoted to retailing and the second floor served as a public meeting hall.

To the south, near Marion Street and South Boulevard, James Scoville and Milton C. Niles began subdividing property in 1863. In 1891, Sidney Niles built the Niles Block at 1101 South Blvd., one block south of Dunlop Brothers, Oak

Park's first bank, which opened in 1887 [4].

The establishment of business districts elsewhere in the village was spurred by residential settlement and the development of train stops along the tracks paralleling Lake Street. Ridgeland, Oak Park and Marion were the three passenger stops on the commuter rail after 1872. Small clusters of shops grew up around passenger depots at each of these locations.

J.P. Willing's carpenter shop was the first business of record at Oak Park Avenue and Lake Street

Scoville was subdividing land east of Oak Park Avenue into residential and commercial lots by 1868. Scoville property south of Lake Street on Oak Park Avenue was reserved for commercial development. The earliest known business establishment at this intersection was J. P. Willing's

carpenter shop, a small, two-story, frame structure originally located on the southwest corner.

In 1899, the Scoville family built a three-story combined commercial and apartment building on the southeast corner of Oak Park Avenue and Lake Street [72]. The building's first tenant was the newly organized Avenue State Bank. Eight years later, the Scovilles built a second building across the street, where Willing's carpenter shop had been [74].

On the southwest corner of the block at 101-105 N. Oak Park Ave., William Goelitz, a plumber, had constructed a two-story brick building in 1888. A grocer occupied the first floor for several decades. Other buildings on the block were constructed between 1888 and 1930.

The extension of this business district to the 100 block of South Oak Park Avenue in the 1900s required the demolition of several homes. By the turn of the century, commercial development near Oak Park Avenue and Lake Street began to rival that of Marion Street.

Farther east along Lake Street was downtown Ridgeland. An 1895 map shows five structures on the northeast corner of Ridgeland

Avenue and Lake Street. The Oak Park directory, historic photos and the proximity of these buildings to the street suggest that they housed businesses.

In 1888 Edmund A. Cummings, a Ridgeland resident and real-estate developer, built a two-story brick building on the north side of Lake Street. Cummings' hall had stores on the ground floor and a public hall above. This structure and the adjacent two-story brick building at 316 Lake St., housing Blase's market, are still standing. The Blase family first opened a grocery on this block in 1892.

Two generations of the Blase family posed around 1914 in front of the second of three buildings the neighborhood market occupied on Lake Street

The commercial buildings within the district were designed in a variety of styles including Romanesque, Queen Anne, Art Nouveau, Prairie and Art Deco.

The financial heyday of the 1920s resulted in some demolition and new construction as well as the remodelling of existing buildings and storefronts.

In reaction to the expansion of businesses and Chicago's continued development along the western border of the city, in 1921 Oak Park enacted a zoning ordinance to limit large-scale commerce and manufacturing. As a result, the local business community is largely comprised of retailers and service providers.

Oak Park's retail establishments prospered when village residents who commuted to work spent their money at home. Between 1927 and 1937 Chicago businesses, including several major retailers like Marshall Fields, opened suburban branches in Oak Park. Before the proliferation of malls, the village was a strategically located shopping mecca for residents of Chicago's western suburbs.

In recent years, an increasing awareness of Oak Park's strong architectural heritage has inspired the restoration of large office buildings and individual store-fronts, including both Scoville buildings on Oak Park Avenue and the Niles building at 1101 South Blvd.

121 S. Maple Ave.

Typical of Italianate style dwellings, this house has both single and paired bracketing under the eaves. Dripboards cap the long, narrow windows. The bay, which extends $2\frac{1}{2}$ stories, displays a variety of trim styles, including thin, decorative columns and panels painted in contrasting colors. The covered porch protects the double doors at the entrance. A small oval window on the north and another bay on the south enhance the otherwise plain side elevations.

Oak Park-River Forest Day Nursery (1926)
Charles E. White, Jr., architect

Despite its size, this large L-shaped building conforms with the residential character of the surrounding neighborhood. The timbered gable roof, brick and stucco exterior and applied wood trim are consistent with Tudor Revival styling.

Established in 1912 with an appropriation from Oak Park's Nineteenth Century Woman's Club, the nursery outgrew its quarters twice in the first three years of operation. In 1915 this lot was purchased. The present facility opened in 1926.

The interior of the building is scaled for children. The fireplace room is decorated with terra-cotta plaques illustrating nursery rhymes. The cabinetry is fashioned with carved animals for door pulls.

H. B. Noyes House (1891)
William J. Van Keuren, architect

3

329 S. Wisconsin Ave.

This house is an essay in the Queen Anne style with highly decorative wood brackets, ornamental balusters and spindle work on the porches, gables, eaves and turret. Often described as "exuberant," Queen Anne designs are characterized by asymmetrical facades, complex plans, large wrap-around porches, projecting bays, highly decorated front gables and corner turrets.

The interior has a carved oak staircase and beam ceiling in the living room. Van Keuren lived at 100 S. Clinton Ave. and designed several other buildings in the district.

Niles Building (1891)
William J. Van Keuren, architect

Van Keuren designed a three-story structure of St. Louis pressed brick and brownstone with projecting, metal bays, restrained Romanesque motifs, stone lintels and carved stone ornament for Sidney S. Niles. Construction costs were estimated at $15,000.

When completed, the building was described by the *West Side Vindicator* as "one conspicuous for size, elegance and substantial construction." The reporter went on to enumerate features, including an elevator, electricity, red oak fixtures, and large display windows of iron and plate glass.

Typical of commercial buildings in the district, the first floor was devoted to commercial and retail space while the second and third floors were offices and apartments. In 1894 a $7,000 addition was constructed to the west of the original structure. The building suffered fires in 1905 and 1907. The original design has been altered over the years, including the addition of ground-floor windows in the once solid masonry wall of the Marion Street facade. The building was restored in 1993.

Playhouse Theater (1913)
Eben Ezra Roberts, architect

When this movie theater opened in 1913, the manager boasted, "there is no handsomer, more comfortable and healthful building." The main floor could accommodate 600 patrons with an additional 100 in the balcony. The auditorium ceiling had a 15-by-30-foot opening with a motorized door. The foyer was paved with mosaic tile, and the building was advertised as fireproof. Although designed as a movie theater, the building had a stage suitable for vaudeville performances.

The exterior of the building is ornamented with rectilinear brickwork. Narrow vertical elements divide the facade. Roberts' geometric ornament is often simpler than that of other Prairie style architects. The structure has undergone numerous renovations and is now an office building.

The Kenton (1897)

Roman brick and contrasting limestone are the prime building materials in this multi-family residence. Roman arches, supported by dwarf columns, provide access to the protected entry. Limestone belt courses divide the second and third floors. A row of dentils runs under the narrow eaves. The polygonal bays on either end of the three-story building terminate in towers at the roofline.

Elwin A. Roser, a commodities broker, developed the site as Oak Park's first apartment hotel and social hall. In the late 1980s, the apartments were renovated, and the building has been restored to near original condition.

The exceptionally large courtyard apartment building around the corner at 932-954 Pleasant Ave. was designed by G. C. Himelblan in 1922.

R. S. Thain House (1892)
Patton and Fisher, architects

210 S. Home Ave.

The play of receding walls and projecting bays across the exterior of this fourteen-room Queen Anne style house creates a highly plastic effect. The shapes and sizes of windows and bays add to the visual variety distinguishing the design.

The simple columns supporting the pediment and roof of the long porch, reappear beneath the deep overhangs protecting the gable windows. The eyebrow form in the end gables of the steeply pitched roof relieves the flatness of the shingled surface.

Each of the first floor rooms includes a window bay with the exception of the kitchen. On the second floor, a small central balcony separates the bays on the west side of the house.

The six-bedroom house cost $11,000 when built. The Thains enjoyed many domestic comforts, including hot-water heat, electricity and indoor plumbing.

John Farson House (1897)
George W. Maher, architect

The clean lines, flat surfaces, massive stone-framed rectilinear windows, broad chimneys and expansive porch openings distinguish this residence from the mansions usually designed for wealthy clients in the late 19th century.

Originally the house was surrounded by seven acres of landscaped grounds and gardens. The large windows on the south facade afforded a wide view of the rose gardens, summer house, tennis courts and greenhouse.

John Farson, a lawyer and banker known for his philanthropic endeavors as well as his penchant for red ties, commissioned Maher to design his home. The name "Pleasant Home" was chosen because the property is located at the corner of Pleasant Street and Home Avenue.

Maher was a contemporary of Frank Lloyd Wright, and shared Wright's interest in developing a uniquely American style of architecture. Maher practiced a "rhythm-motif theory," establishing two or three design elements that were repeated throughout the building. This concept is expressed at Pleasant Home in the geometric shape of a "tray" framed by a spray of honeysuckle, the arrowhead, the lion's head, and the interplay of squares and circles throughout the building.

A rolled steel fence with an elongated "tray" design encloses the north and east sides of the estate. The arrowhead motif on the imposing urns flanking the entrance is repeated under the eaves of the house. The drain scuppers on the exterior wall of the front porch are decorated with lions' heads as are the brackets on the third-floor dormers. The tray wrapped in honeysuckle, as well as the circle and square, are basic elements in the design of the art glass windows on either side of the front door.

Pleasant Home is the realization of Maher's belief that a house should have massiveness and

solidity to express substantiality, an ideal he presented in an 1887 speech "Originality in American Architecture," delivered to the Chicago Architectural Sketch Club.

After Farson's death in 1910, Herbert Mills, a manufacturer of vending machines, purchased the property for $175,000. The Mills family lived here until 1929. In 1939, the village's park district bought the property for $202,000.

The house is undergoing restoration and is open for guided tours at regularly scheduled times. For tour information, call (708)383-2654. The Historical Society of Oak Park and River Forest is located on the second floor. Call (708) 848-6755 for information.

Garland House (ca. 1852)

9

241 S. Home Ave.

Originally constructed on Lake Street near Forest Avenue, this house was moved to its present location after 1855 and is believed to be the oldest surviving dwelling in the district. The original section of the house was Federal style. Early modifications include the addition at the rear as well as the veranda. Stucco was applied to the frame in 1910.

The property was owned for 60 years by Abraham Edmunds, a millworker and cabinetmaker. He trimmed the sitting rooms in birch, hickory and sycamore and is responsible for the oak front stairway. Edmunds' work can be seen in Pleasant Home, the Walnut Room at Marshall Fields, the Continental Bank and the Field Museum of Natural History.

Alex Kryl House (1908)
Alex Kryl, builder

The street facade of this two-flat is constructed of brown face brick, which modestly trims the common-brick side walls. The relief that dominates the entryway was executed by the builder, a sculptor who emigrated from Eastern Europe. The subject of the relief is inspired by his own life and family.

Kryl chose trees and animals native to the midwest in his representation of the hunt. The woman wearing a scarf carved on the front pillar is a likeness of his mother, while the man with a moustache on the urn is a portrait of his brother.

Kryl also worked on St. Catherine of Siena Church, the soldier's monument at the Cicero town hall and Rosary College in River Forest.

404 S. Home Ave.

George Smith House (1895-1898)
Frank Lloyd Wright, architect

Steeply pitched, double-sloped roofs and shingle siding suggest this house may have been adapted from a group of affordable homes Frank Lloyd Wright designed in 1895 for Charles Roberts. The original project was never executed.

The structure seems out of context with others Wright designed in the late 1890s, especially in the use of double-hung windows with diamond-shaped leaded glass rather than casement windows with geometric art glass patterns. The broad, overhanging eaves, hidden entrance and board-and-batten exterior are more consistent with contemporary structures by Wright.

George Smith was a buyer for Marshall Fields, and in 1894 lived in a larger Queen Anne style house at 218 S. Grove Ave.

12

Charles W. Austin House (1905)
Charles E. White, Jr., architect

This simple, gabled roof, Prairie style house of wood-trimmed stucco shows the influence of the architect's employer, Frank Lloyd Wright. The watertable creates a strong base. Two parallel, wooden stringcourses extend the length of the front facade, wrapping around the porch. Wood trim on the second floor frames and unifies the window sections.

When White designed this dwelling for Charles Austin, a mathematics teacher, the architect had not yet formed a personal style. He designed a number of houses in the district, an apartment building at 24-32 W. Washington Blvd. and the 1933 Oak Park post office.

Frank W. Hall House (1904)
Eben Ezra Roberts, architect

The linear detailing, emphasis on rectangular forms in mass and surface, and low hipped roof with wide eaves define the Prairie style character of this building. Despite Roberts' strong preference for stucco, he used wood siding on the first floor of this house designed for a lumber dealer. The broad porch, weighty corner piers and narrow spindles extending below the porch deck lend an air of formality to the front entrance. Compare this design with 321 S. Clinton Ave. built two years earlier.

321 S. Clinton Ave.

Isaac N. Conrad House (1902)
Eben Ezra Roberts, architect

In contrast with the ornamented Queen Anne or Stick style houses of the mid to late 19th century, the design of this residence exemplifies the new simplicity, formality and symmetry distinguishing Oak Park houses around 1900. The rusticated stone foundation and large fluted columns recall historical styles, but the rectangular masses and geometric detailing reflect an interest in Prairie style principles.

The clapboard exterior is divided by a prominent stringcourse, and windowed dormers project from the steep hipped roof on all sides.

308 S. Clinton Ave.

Probably constructed from builders' plan books, the straight-forward design of this house is enlivened by decorative detailing. The clapboard structure rests on a rubblestone foundation. The long porch railing is composed of turned spindles and columns that support the porch roof. Mitered lengths of wood face the front gable and form a background for the decorative sunburst. The small, rectangular second-floor windows rest on equally decorative wood-framed flower motifs.

C. R. Heneage House (1912)
Hodgkins and Burrows, architects

This 2½-story residence is one of the few examples of Tudor Revival style architecture in the historic district. Architectural features include the steeply sloped, dominant gable, smaller secondary gables, multiple chimney stacks and upper-level casement windows with numerous small panes of glass. The play of curved and vertical elements in the half-timbering softens the design and echoes the rounded opening to the porch.

The house was built by Krogman Brothers for $2,000. It has been converted to a two-flat.

(ca. 1873)

211 S. Clinton Ave.

Depicted on an 1873 map of Oak Park, this Italianate residence originally was a modest-sized house with a rooftop cupola. The enclosed porch and rear section of the house are additions. The Lemont limestone foundation was carefully matched in the remodelling process.

The low hipped roof, bracketed eaves and tall, narrow windows are typical Italianate features. When built, the house probably had a front and back parlor, dining room and lean-to kitchen on the first floor, with four bedrooms on the second floor. Most of the interior woodwork is pine with the exception of a mahogany bannister on the front stairs.

E. F. Burton Rowhouses (1892)
James H. Willett and Alfred F. Pashley, architects

This grouping of five attached residences illustrates the variety of forms and details typically found on Queen Anne style detached houses. Despite their apparent diversity, the units are related through the symmetry of the two end-unit bays, the pattern of dormers and the continuous eaves. The varied materials, eclectic architectural vocabulary and distinctive entrances create a lively facade. The corner unit with its Romanesque entrance and corner oriel is particularly striking.

The village contains four other rowhouse groupings:
313-319 S. Maple Ave., 100-110 S. Home Ave.,
115-121 N. Kenilworth Ave. and 200-208 Forest Ave.

19

John I. Jones House (1897)
H. G. Fiddelke, architect

When compared with Queen Anne houses of the preceding decade, the design of this house reflects the transition to more angular forms and restrained surfaces. The bays, gables, dormers, wrap-around porch and windows of varied size and shape remain, but the dramatic contrasts and excesses of Queen Anne styling have been checked.

The foundation is rusticated stone. The exterior of the first and second floor is clapboard, while shingles face the third floor gables. The bracketing and decorative tracery of the porch pediment are repeated above the second-and third-floor window groupings.

Wesley A. Arnold House (1888)
Wesley A. Arnold, architect

130 S. Kenilworth Ave.

This Victorian Romanesque home attracted notice in the *Oak Park Reporter* of October 12, 1888. "Mr. Arnold will soon begin the erection of a residence for himself on Prairie Avenue, near Pleasant, which will be quite novel in some of its features. The first story will be of mottled sandstone, with red trimmings, while the second will be of purple slate. The house will cost about $4,000 and will be one of the most attractive on the south side."

The variety of surface textures and stones combined in this house contribute to its unique design. A round, windowed dormer creates the effect of a small turret. The horseshoe arch framing the entrance and the art glass window are other notable architectural elements.

Arnold also designed the house at 134 S. Kenilworth Ave., which has Romanesque features and textures similar to those of his own home but rendered in wood.

Skeen Flats (1892)

The textures of the rusticated, greystone blocks and carved friezes and keystones found in this duplex contrast markedly with the smooth surfaces of the porch members. Dentils define the upper edge of the exterior wall, and a central stone ridge dividing the gabled roof indicates a party wall below. The unit at 249 is a two-story home, while 247 is a two-flat.

> *The corner playground at Grove Avenue and Randolph Street before 1902 was the site of a passenger station on the Chicago, Harlem and Batavia train line, also known as the dummy line.*

235 S. Grove Ave.

With the exception of the front porches, the opposing houses at 234 and 235 S. Grove Ave. are mirror images. Probably built from the same floor plan, the buildings exhibit the steeply pitched roof, prominent gable, curved and rectangular bays, and large front porch common to Queen Anne style residences. Ornamental wood shingling on the front gable adds pattern and texture to the exterior wall surface.

22

C. R. Blanchard House (1894)

213 S. Grove Ave.

23

This residence is a clear example of Stick style architecture. The frame structure is accented with wood trim. The exterior is clad primarily in bevel siding, with zones of fishscale shingles separating the windows. The window casing is made up of multiple pieces of trim. Brackets support the turret, and fretwork accents the gable front.

J. I. Jones House (1887)
H. G. Fiddelke, architect

209 S. Grove Ave.

This house, built when "nooks and crannies" were the height of fashion, embodies the varied forms and surface irregularity of eclectic Victorian design. Contrasting wood trim joins the corner turret to the front gable and extends across the front to the rectangular bay. The projecting front gable is supported on horseshoe-shaped arches. Turned columns support the roof of the broad, open porch.

25

John A. Seaman House (1894)
H. G. Fiddelke and Frank Ellis, architects

The impressive scale and prominent corner site of this house command attention in a block of distinctive Victorian houses. Consistent with changing taste in the late 19th century, the form and massing of the house are simpler than many neighboring structures. Originally painted white, the house must have contrasted with more popular, colorful paint schemes.

The house retains the broad front porch, entrance gable, roof dormers and bays of Queen Anne style houses. The balustrade that ran along the upper edge of the French mansard roof has been removed. The middle dormer on the east elevation is a later addition.

The richly detailed interior is trimmed in exotic woods. Ellis was responsible for the interior millwork. The kitchen was outfitted with every convenience, including running water, a hot water tank and ice box.

A native of New York and cooper by trade, John A. Seaman owned most of the block. During construction, the family lived in the house immediately to the north. The total cost was $17,000, a substantial sum at the time. In 1897 Seaman moved to 200 S. Grove Ave., a house also designed by Fiddelke.

(1913)
John S. Van Bergen, architect

106 S. Grove Ave.

Designed as a speculative venture, this house
demonstrates the typical features of Prairie style
buildings, such as the low hipped roof with broad
overhanging eaves, horizontal grouping of casement windows, contrasting wood trim and hidden
entrance. The plan was not unique and was
simply reversed for a house on Fair Oaks Avenue.
George Hemingway commissioned the house
and planned to sell it when completed, but a buyer
could not be found until 1924.

The oldest Catholic church in Oak Park, St. Edmund and the nearby school are neighborhood landmarks. The design of this imposing English Gothic Revival structure includes, a stainless steel steeple surmounted by a Celtic cross, tall traceried windows, embattled coping, cruciform plan and buttressed walls of Indiana limestone. The marble carving over the entrance depicts St. Edmund of Canterbury.

On the interior, the arches and ribs of the groined ceiling are supported on eight pillars. The large stained-glass windows, commissioned from the Zeidler firm in Munich, depict scenes from the Gospels. The sanctuary decorations, completed in 1943, include paintings by art students in Vienna. The interior decor reflects the early parish's struggle to retain the cherished traditions of its multiethnic membership.

When the parish's founder, Father John C. Code, came to the village, religious intolerance forced him to say his first Mass in an abandoned barn. He appealed

St. Edmund Church (1909)
Henry J. Schlacks, architect

to John Farson, a neighbor with a large estate at 217 S. Home Ave., to allow the church to host a fundraising event on his land. Farson, who was not a Catholic, not only agreed but gave a gracious speech welcoming some 2,000 guests. His actions inspired greater public tolerance, and the lawn fete helped raise $3,000. In 1907 the lot was purchased and the building completed in 1910.

St. Edmund School (1917)
Henry J. Schlacks, architect

208 S. Oak Park Ave.

Modeled after the Palais du Justice in Rouen, France, the school is the best example of French Gothic Revival design in Oak Park. The octagonal bay contains three traceried windows along with three dormer windows, each flanked by lances and defined with sculptured moldings. A four-foot-high, perforated railing crowns the cornice and encircles the building. Buttresses terminating in pinnacles rise between gargoyles to support the cornice. A marble relief depicting Christ blessing children fills the niche above the west entrance. The Indiana limestone exterior matches that of the church. The building was dedicated on October 14, 1917.

29

LuViola Apartment Building (1914)
A. F. Colcord, architect

The three-story brick structure containing 18 apartments cost $90,000 when built. The tiled, entry pavilions, supported on brackets, are similar to architectural features incorporated into the California designs of Henry and Charles Greene. The contrasting stone and brickwork establish a geometric pattern on the exterior walls.

The apartment interiors were designed with beam ceilings, mahogany buffets and ceramic tile bathrooms. In 1978 the building was converted to condominiums.

The larger but contemporary building at 801-809 W. Washington Blvd. with its projecting bays and balconies, third-floor, clad stucco ornament and shallow entrance gables demonstrates the stylistic variety in apartment building design within the district. The setback conforms with the lot line established by neighboring single-family homes.

Oak Park Arms (1921)
Roy T. France, architect

408 S. Oak Park Ave.

A former apartment hotel, this Oak Park landmark is now a residence for senior citizens. The lighter stone of the ground level is used ornamentally on the upper floors where it divides the facade and accents or frames window openings. The structure contained ninety-three apartments and cost $600,000 when built.

The Washington Boulevard entrance and terrace were added in 1927. The following year, William G. Krieg designed the five-story addition to the south.

Michael Breen Apartments (1911)

711-713 W. Washington Blvd.

This 2½-story, brick apartment building incorporates the features of a typical large single-family residence of the period. Dressed limestone wall caps, capitals and bands accent the exterior along with the open-work brick designs of the porch fronts. Dentils and brackets define the juncture between the wall and overhanging eaves. Two large attic dormers overlooking the street and four additional dormers on both the east and west facade expand the interior space and provide natural light to the residents.

Euclid Avenue United Methodist Church (1921)
Eben Ezra Roberts, architect

Wesley Arnold, a member of the congregation and church steward, designed a red sandstone chapel for members of the Euclid Avenue Methodist Episcopal Church. In 1899 the first story was built. During the previous year, the 35 members of the congregation had met in an abandoned suburban railroad station, which, according to a local newspaper account, was "the most unique sanctuary to be found in Chicago or any of its suburbs." In 1906 a second story was constructed and the chapel completed.

In 1921 construction began on a larger Norman Gothic church, which was completed in 1922. The simple formality of the limestone exterior is enriched by a large traceried and stained-glass Gothic window above the entrance. Small Gothic windows of variegated gold glass line the side walls.

William Taylor House (ca. 1907)

The simple geometric masses and symmetrical arrangement of windows and decorative elements distinguish this large, dignified family home. The design adapts many Prairie style elements to the basic foursquare plan, including strong horizontal lines, broad overhanging eaves and a stringcourse dividing the first and second floors. Stylistic features of the main house were modified and restated in the design of the coach house.

The house had its own generator and like many Oak Park buildings was supplied with the Yaryan system of hot-water heat piped from a central plant at Euclid Avenue and North Boulevard.

An unusual combination of architectural elements align this house with no single genre. Prairie style features include the smooth stucco exterior walls, wood trim and horizontal window groupings. The curved roof parapet on the side elevations and the arched dormer on the front are eccentric variants. The house at 331 S. Euclid Ave., also by Roberts, has a similar dormer. The continuous horizontal bands wrapping the upper wall, porch roof and piers seem to presage the linear styling of art deco design.

Arthur J. Lloyd House (1910)
Eben Ezra Roberts, architect

34

Roy Davis House (1940)
Charles Kristen, architect

Of more recent date than most structures in the vicinity, this house is the sole representative of Art Deco residential design in the district. Features consistent with the streamlined aesthetic include, the smooth exterior wall accented by horizontal decorative brick courses, flat roof and stepped silhouette with narrow coping. The house was constructed at a cost of $18,000.

35

201 S. Wesley Ave.

Wooden trim of varied shape and color lends a playful exuberance to this Stick style house. The veranda balusters combine flat and rounded forms paralleling those on a smaller scale accenting the porch roofline. Polygonal and square bays extend from three sides of the house. The gables of the steeply pitched roof are framed by the simple geometric design of the rake boards.

Shingles, applied boards and sunbursts enliven the gables and horizontal siding on the exterior walls.

H. H. Morgan House (1887)
Cicero Hines, architect

229 S. Wesley Ave.

The basic symmetrical form of this house is offset by the varied shape, size and placement of windows and trim on the front facade. The bay on the second floor exhibits an unusual combination of decorative shingles, curved wood trim and brackets crowned by an overhanging gable.

The curve motif is expanded in the design of the first floor porch roof and in the horseshoe-shaped, shingled surrounds of the front window and entranceway.

37

W. G. Gilbert House (1911)
A.F. Rusy, architect

38

626 W. Washington Blvd.

A generously scaled variant of the bungalow, this house is one of several district buildings suggesting the Spanish Revival style. Character is achieved through the stucco facade, tile roof and bracketed porch eaves. The steeply pitched center gable provides a striking contrast to the low, horizontal lines of the roof.

Fenwick High School (1928)
Wilfrid Edwards Anthony, architect

The three-story, block-long building was designed as a Catholic high school to serve the western suburbs. The Massachusetts granite exterior walls, massive wooden entrance doors and casement windows contribute to the formal English Gothic styling.

The stone facade is trimmed in contrasting smooth and light-colored Indiana limestone about the front entrance. Carved reliefs and statues ornament the exterior, including crests flanked by carved visages of Dominican saints. The cornerstone of the tower, which was designed as a studio for art classes, bears the shield of the Dominican order.

Originally known as the Dominican High School, the institution was renamed in honor of Edward Dominic Fenwick, the friar who established the Dominican order in the United States.

Good Shepherd Lutheran Church, 611 Randolph St., was designed by Bird and Hotchkiss in 1941. The red brick, Colonial Williamsburg style building has a classical portico, arched windows and square central tower.

Luther Conant "Quadrangle" Apartments (1907)
Eben Ezra Roberts, architect

108-118 S. East Ave.

This building is an innovative departure from the flat-roofed, boxlike design of conventional urban apartment buildings. The combination of alternating bays and open porches, pitched roofs, wood-trimmed gables and contrasting surface textures earned high praise in the local press, which described the building as one "in harmony" with Oak Park ideals.

Roberts designed three buildings amid generous lawns and circular pathways. The plan observed the setback established by private, single-family homes on the block. Each building, constructed at an approximate cost of $19,000, had six, seven-room apartments. An early advertisement for the building noted every room had a window opening directly to light and air.

213-215 S. Elmwood Ave.

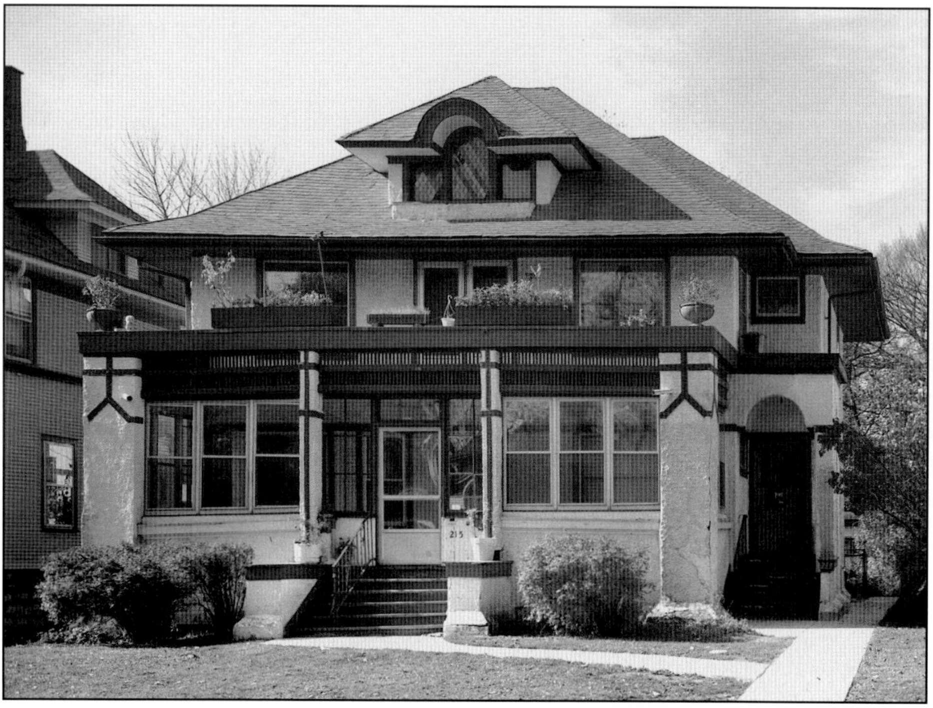

A. H. Hopkins House (1905)
Eben Ezra Roberts, architect

The symmetrical facade of this large stucco dwelling conceals two separate residences. Like many of Roberts' Prairie style residential designs, the building comprises a foursquare plan, hipped roof, broad eaves and wood-trimmed stucco exterior. The doorway to the north leads to the upper-level apartment.

Construction costs were $5,000. An addition was built in 1927. Roberts designed the house at 209-211 S. Elmwood Ave., which is also a two-flat.

Rose Kavana Apartments (1909)
Eben Ezra Roberts, architect

E. E. Roberts was adept at disguising two flats as single-family homes in order to answer local concerns about increasing residential density without sacrificing the character of the neighborhood. The identical window locations on the first and second floors indicating twin floor plans and a discreetly placed second door to the right of the main entrance reveal the true residential function of this building.

The simple hipped roof, broad eaves, and stucco surface with horizontal trim and geometric ornament are consistent with the overall Prairie character of the structure. In 1974 the building was converted into a single-family home.

(1904)
Lawrence Buck, architect

Picturesque features of this cottage
include a steeply pitched roof,
gables and arched doorway. The
simple massing of the building, the
grouping of casement windows
and the smooth, stucco surface,
however, demonstrate the
architect's interest in Prairie
school design. The house cost
$2500 to build. Buck distilled
Prairie elements in the design of
a handful of houses in Oak Park.

Our Lady Immaculate Church (1920)
William Drummond, architect

410 W. Washington Blvd.

This building was commissioned by members of the Second Presbyterian Church when the congregation outgrew smaller quarters on this site. The original building remains on the north side of the lot.

The east and south facades are identical with two entrances forming a corner at Ridgeland Avenue and Washington Boulevard. Brick pilasters mark the north and west ends of the building and define the center window of the bays. Diamond-shaped, leaded-glass windows terminate in decorative hood molds. Patterned brick and carved limestone were used as exterior ornament. The Roman Catholic Latin Rite congregation purchased the property in 1989.

(1903)

321, 325 and 328 S. Ridgeland Ave.

These three brick cottages are variations on a single theme. Similar in form, plan and siting, they contribute to a unified streetscape. The most obvious distinction among the buildings is the differing size and shape of the second-floor windows.

Originally owned by Mrs. Taylor, the houses were probably rented to families with modest household incomes. Each 1½-story dwelling was constructed for $1,800. The front porches and landscaping have all changed over time.

(1907)
Eben Ezra Roberts, architect

224 S. Ridgeland Ave.

The houses on the east side of the 200 block of South Ridgeland Avenue were all commissioned as a speculative venture by A. D. Orvis. Each structure has a distinct character, but together they suggest a harmonious community of homes, especially when compared to a block of highly individualized Queen Anne residences.

The front elevation of this house displays an unusual vertical panel framing the windows and projecting beyond the roofline to include the dormer. This strong vertical element is countered by the broad, horizontal, open porch. The exterior is clad in narrow, wood siding, an exception to the architect's usual practice.

F. Dore General Store (1870s)

115 S. Ridgeland Ave.

Originally located at the northeast corner of Ridgeland Avenue and Lake Street, this building served as a general store. The back room of the first floor became the first Ridgeland school, while the second floor served as a town meeting hall.

As often seen in small, wood-frame commercial structures of this era, the exterior walls carry the floor load, eliminating the need for internal supports and center walls. The selling floor was thus completely open to display merchandise and accommodate crowds.

In 1902, the building was moved to its current location, placed on a new foundation and converted into a simplified Victorian residence for J. Timm. It was remodeled again in the late 1970s.

48

(1923)
J. J. Jameson, architect

These long, low storefronts have been constructed of masonry and highlighted with individual terra cotta panels above the entrances. Identical terra cotta ornamental motifs can be found on a handful of Chicago storefronts. The panels were probably stock design from a local manufacturer. The original storefronts are intact with clear glass display windows and small squares of prismatic glass above. George Prassas commissioned the buildings at a cost of $90,000.

Querin H. Cook House (1914)
John S. Van Bergen, architect

Despite its modest size, this Prairie style house includes many features found in larger, better-known houses designed by Frank Lloyd Wright in the village. The simple stucco exterior is accented with horizontal bands of wood. A shallow pitched roof with broad eaves shelters the clean rectilinear form of the building. The open floor plan and window groupings permit a generous amount of light to reach the interior spaces. The raised casement windows preserve the privacy of the residents. The house was built by Benson and Peterson for $4,000.

(1925)
Roy T. France, architect

237-241 W. Washington Blvd.

This large building demonstrates how zoning and building codes affected the design of apartment buildings in Oak Park. An interest in protecting the well-being of tenants inspired the development of central courtyards that allowed light and air to circulate throughout the building. More typical urban apartment buildings were designed as solid blocks pierced by light wells. The courtyards were often partially closed from the street to create a semi-private yard for the enjoyment of the residents.

Many of the apartment buildings found along this street have projecting bays that break up the facade, reducing the overwhelming mass of the wall. Roof treatments vary; in this case a parapet masks the flatness of the roof.

51

418 S. Harvey Ave.

W. H. Griffith House (1914)
John S. Van Bergen, architect

The pure geometry of this residence is typical of the architect who believed, "Good proportions mean good architecture; simplicity means good taste in all forms of art." The stucco exterior with horizontal wood trim, windows grouped in bands, broad chimney, wide eaves and recessed entrance are notable Prairie style elements.

The large, enclosed porch anchors the two-story block of the house. Open but covered porches, located at the front of the house on narrow lots or at the side on long lots, were an integral component of Van Bergen's residential designs. In most cases, the porches were later enclosed.

Van Bergen designed houses with innovative and practical features, such as built-ins with pass-through shelves and drawers between adjoining rooms, and ceiling vents that opened into chimneys or dormers to promote circulation.

Glen Ellyn Apartments (1912)
H. H. Richards, architect

In contrast to the courtyard apartment buildings found elsewhere in the village, here a straightforward solution was found to ensure residents adequate light and air. Each unit was designed with a porch overlooking the large front lawn. These projecting porches also serve to divide the street facade visually into smaller units. Contrasting stone courses and geometric accents enrich the brick exterior and frame the entrances. The tile roof exists only on the street facade, disguising the typical flat roof elsewhere on the building.

Oak Dale Apartments (1907)

An L-shaped building design was yet another solution to provide ample light and ventilation to apartment dwellers. The building is sited close to the sidewalk, establishing a formidable block and atypically ignoring the residential setback.

An open courtyard is hidden from view behind the building. Each apartment has a view of the street and a view of the courtyard, with the added benefit of cross-ventilation. A 1907 advertisement for the Oak Dale declared, "The dweller in an apartment is entitled to the same conveniences and to as good light as the man who lives in a house."

The exceptional simplicity of the existing, original cornice is noteworthy. Terra cotta medallions relieve the single-plane cove. The original courtyard, was landscaped as a private garden, but has been converted into a parking lot.

54

Lake Street Elevated Railway Company (1903)
W. Carbys Zimmerman, architect

This 3½-story, brick block with stone detailing was once an electrical generating substation powering the Lake Street elevated trains from Harlem Avenue in Oak Park east to Pulaski Avenue in Chicago.

The front section of the building is divided into three floors while the back is one large, open space. The details of the facade, with its punched window openings, narrow stone courses and brick coursework above and below the third-floor window openings, emphasize the simple mass and clear geometric form of the building.

The structure was used for storage until it was abandoned in 1967. A local sculptor has renovated the building for use as a studio and residence.

H. W. Austin Apartments (1910)
H. H. Richards, architect

The two-story apartment building retains the vertical
scale of neighboring structures and respects the
setback of individual homes along the street. The
apartments are grouped around a shared, tile-roofed
entrance. The L-shaped plan provides a private
space at the rear of the property devoted to lawn
and garages. H. W. Austin, the first owner, advertised
the apartments as four- and five-room units in 1910.
Henry Hogans was the builder.

Marjorie Maddock House (1922)
William C. Presto, architect

301 S. Lombard Ave.

The southern California designs of architects Henry
and Charles Greene were the source of the Craftsman
style bungalow. The 1½-story layout, low hipped
roof, wide eaves and exposed roof rafters conform
with the style. The original roof was probably tile
or wood shingles. Pattern books and magazines
popularized the bungalow design from about 1905
through the end of the '20s. The multi-paned windows
contribute to the cottage-like character of this house,
which cost $9,000 to construct.

J. Moffett House (ca. 1910)
N. E. Palmer, architect

The low roof with curved stucco eaves, grouping of leaded-glass windows, and geometric wood trim are Prairie style features applied to the design of this bungalow. The side entry would later become a common variant of the basic bungalow form.

This property was constructed by W. E. Blum as a model for a residential development that never materialized.

(1929)
Henry J. Appelbach, architect

415-427 S. Taylor Ave.

The unusual ornament of this courtyard building recalls French Renaissance architecture. Cut stone and terra cotta highlight the yellow brick exterior. The apartments all have bays, and the E-shaped plan provides each unit with two and sometimes three exposures. Steel casement windows open out onto large, airy courtyards and the front units have french doors.

Designed with many luxurious amenities, the interiors featured tiled kitchens and baths, white-oak floors, built-in niches and maids quarters in the larger units. The original cost of construction was $400,000. The Oak Leaf Building Corporation was the first owner.

J. W. Farr House (1908)
J. W. Farr, builder

430 S. Taylor Ave.

The plain stucco walls, angled front pilasters and side entrance of this house are reminiscent of the designs of Glasgow architect Charles R. Mackintosh. The ribbon casement windows of the exterior walls and dormer, and the tile roof contribute to the Arts and Crafts character of the design.

Farr, a plaster contractor, designed and built his own home as a demonstration of his talents. The building cost $3,000. The stucco fence was added when the apartment building was constructed to the north, shortly after the house was completed.

60

St. Catherine of Siena Church (1930-1934)
Joseph McCarthy, architect

This large Gothic Revival style building dominates the surrounding landscape. The church is most noted for its soaring height and large French Gothic windows with stone tracery superimposed on the stained glass.

The grey Plymouth granite and Indiana limestone exterior of the building is invested with symbols of the Catholic faith, including the coat of arms of St. Catherine above the main door. A slender copper spire rises above the slate roof at the crossing.

The arches, vaults and piers of the structure remain exposed, consistent with Gothic design. The interior includes an altar of solid blocks of Carrara marble.

In 1889, thirty-three families established the parish of St. Catherine. The first Mass was celebrated in the Oaks Club at Waller Avenue and Lake Street. By year's end, the congregation had moved into a newly built Shingle style church at Washington Boulevard and Parkside Avenue. In 1917 they moved to larger quarters, a combined brick church and school at Washington Boulevard and Humphrey Avenue. Construction began on the present building in 1930. The church cost $360,000.

W. A. Pillinger House (ca. 1910)
W. A. Pillinger, builder

61

This imposing residence is a unique synthesis of Prairie style elements, traditional Queen Anne layout and starkly modern forms. Prairie style references include the hipped roof, broad, overhanging eaves and ribbon windows of the first floor facade. The tower and asymmetrical massing are typical of Queen Anne designs, but the deceptively modern appearance of this house results from the striking simplicity of its form and surfaces.

Johnson Brothers Apartments (1916)

62

The projecting bays of this U-shaped apartment building progressively increase in depth and help to visually reduce the size of the courtyard. Horizontal stone courses and quoins accent the brick exterior. The terra cotta medallions were probably purchased through a catalog. The 30-unit building was constructed for about $100,000.

First National Bank (1920)

412 N. Austin Blvd.

The building exemplifies the Classical Revival styling found in many midwestern banks of this period. Bankers hoped the design of a building would convey a sense of strength and conservative values to their patrons.

Despite numerous remodelings, the original design is apparent in the dressed stone facade, large, plate glass windows and imposing entrance framed by pilasters. The name of the bank is still engraved above the door. A glass and iron wall separated the tellers from the public space of the lobby.

First National Bank of Oak Park had been organized as the Austin Avenue Trust and Savings Bank in 1911. Henry Pillinger was the first president. In 1930 the bank entered receivership and closed. Currently a medical clinic, the building also has been used as a funeral home and art studio.

West Suburban Hospital (1912)
Eben Ezra Roberts, architect

The office of E. E. Roberts proposed this elevation for West Suburban Hospital in March 1912.

This local institution has undergone many changes since construction. The concept of a modern community-based hospital was first discussed by a group of local physicians in 1911. The original building was a simple, red brick block with stone quoins and base. The design was amended before the hospital was completed in 1914, and the entrance gained emphasis during the construction phase. Additions and renovations to modernize the facility have changed the exterior. Remodeling projects in 1926, the 1950s, 1960 and 1982 have doubled the hospital's size and substantially altered the original building, as well.

A. J. Curtis House (1921)
H. K. Holsman, architect

301 N. Taylor Ave.

The concrete block exterior of this single-family home is unusual for residential designs of the period. The blocks simulate the mass and substance of stone, but would have been considerably less expensive. The house may have been an experimental model.

The entrance detailing and banding of the second-floor window sills are consistent with Classical Revival designs, as are the arched windows, fluted columns and symmetrical openings of the first floor. The house was built by W. J. Johnson for $20,000.

(1913)   George R Davis, builder

66

The uniformity of these buildings is their most notable architectural feature. The east side of the street is lined with simple, one-story stucco bungalows, while the west side is composed of two-story stucco foursquares.

George R. Davis constructed the bungalows in 1913 for Raymond G. Hancock or M. R. Wadsworth as an apparent speculative venture. Each bungalow cost $3,000 to construct and was listed for sale between $5,250 and $5,750.

John Carne House (ca. 1870)

144 N. Cuyler Ave.

This vernacular cottage is one of the earliest surviving houses in the district. The wood-frame building is enlivened with Italianate gable brackets and a bay with tall arched windows on the side. Other early cottages stand at 418 and 419 N. Cuyler Ave. and at 139 and 143 N. Harvey Ave.

171 N. Cuyler Ave.

Faith United Methodist Church (1902)
Charles Frost and Alfred Granger, architects

In a 1914 newspaper account, Frost described his design of the Cuyler Avenue Methodist Church as a "free adaptation of the Gothic style as exemplified in some of the less pretentious country churches of England." The Norman Gothic building is constructed of rough-hewn and carved red granite. The stone, according to the architect, required extreme restraint in mass and detail, producing a building "as simple, as humble even, as a church can be; owing its effect to its simplicity and its walliness."

Contrast and ornament were thus reserved for the three main gables where tudor detailing accents the plain stucco surfaces. The original roof was probably slate.

The Cuyler Avenue Methodist Church was founded in 1900. Ground was broken for the structure in 1902, and the building was completed in 1914 at a cost of $20,000.

(1912)
Frederick R. Schock, architect

The street facade of this apartment building makes a strong decorative statement. The geometric, terra cotta ornament, reminiscent of Louis Sulllivan's designs, contrasts dramatically with the uniform red brick ground and is consistent with Prairie style designs elsewhere in the district.

Similar decorative details were incorporated in the design of the adjacent store, establishing a continuity of designs on the west and east facades of this corner building. E. A. Cummings, a prominent realtor, commissioned the structures.

Pilgrim Congregational Church (1889)
Normand S. Patton, architect

This church joins the rambling, irregular plan of the Queen Anne style with the highly textured, exterior surface of the Shingle style. The building's rough Illinois limestone base is trimmed with red brick. The upper section is wood frame. The gables are faced with wood shingles, panels and carved wood ornament.

The window tracery is wood, while the sills are terra cotta. The arched windows have abstract, geometric patterns rather than the figurative designs found in many churches of this period.

The main entrance was originally on Scoville Avenue. The asymmetrical plan and massing produce the "picturesque" effect popular in the late 19th century.

The Ridgeland Congregational Society first met in 1874 in the local train station. The members formed the Second Congregational Church in 1888, and constructed the south chapel for $8,000 on land donated by James Scoville. The chapel, designed by Normand S. Patton, was consecrated on April 26, 1889. The building program continued with a $55,000 addition, designed by Patton and Miller and dedicated on March 25, 1899.

Medical Arts Building (1929)
Roy J. Hotchkiss, architect

715 Lake St.

The continuous stone piers and recessed spandrels of this Art Deco style building make the 109-foot office tower seem exceptionally tall. The design is organized symmetrically about the main entrance and extends for several bays along the side elevations. The simpler, brick side walls were designed with the same pattern of continuous piers and recessed spandrels. The building was constructed of a steel skeleton with reinforced concrete slab floors.

Village officials denied C. B. Scoville a construction permit for the proposed building, which exceeded local height restrictions by 29 feet. Scoville persuaded his opponents that additional height was required to house the mechanical systems and to allow for retail space in the building. He instructed the architect to "spare no effort or expense" to create a noteworthy design. The building cost $250,000.

Scoville Building (1899)
Patton, Fisher and Miller, architects

James Scoville died in 1893, but his family continued to develop this section of the village for commercial purposes. After ten years of deliberation, they built the first of two large office buildings at this intersection.

The tile roof, stepped Flemish gables and projecting bays with individual cornices create a strong visual presence on this prominent corner lot. The commercial structure contains shops on the first floor and apartments above, continuing the pattern of mixed use established in early commercial building's elsewhere in the district.

The design was inspired by the town hall in Frankfort, Germany. Eben Ezra Roberts designed the 1901 addition. Roy Hotchkiss redesigned the storefronts in 1929.

Cicero Gas Company Building (1893)
Patton and Fisher, architects

The compact mass of this combined-use structure with its large corner tower and half-timbered gable commands a place in this commercial streetscape. Large, low arches and massive columns frame the first-floor entrance facade recalling H. H. Richardson's East Coast designs. A second arched entrance and projecting bays along Hunter Court to the north relate the building's street and alley facades.

The design provided commercial space on the lower level and apartments above. In 1925 the structure was remodeled by Roy Hotchkiss, and in the 1940s was used as a rooming house.

73

74

129-151 N. Oak Park Ave.

Scoville Building (1907)
Eben Ezra Roberts, architect

In contrast to the commercial building across the street modeled on earlier European forms, the second Scoville building displays distinctly Prairie style elements.

Strong, contrasting horizontal stone bands separate the first-floor storefronts from the upper-

level offices. The brick facade is articulated by stepped piers at the corner and the second- and third-floor window groupings. The low hipped roof and broad overhanging eaves are typical Prairie style features. The main entrance is recessed, providing space for the elaborate glass canopy and mosaic tile floor.

The building, which was previously the home of Gilmore's Department Store and the local Masonic lodge, was restored in 1986.

The Gothic Revival style of this structure originates in the 14th-and 15th-century designs of English and French churches. The present building with its unusual polygonal transepts was constructed in 1917, following the general groundlines of an earlier structure destroyed by fire when lightning struck the steeple. The building incorporates some of the stones from the original church, along with stone salvaged from another church destroyed by fire in Chicago. The bell was saved and reinstalled in the new tower.

The rusticated Joliet limestone of the facade contrasts with the smoother Indiana limestone trimming the doors and windows. A large rose window was designed above the south entrance. On the interior, carved wood rafters support the slate roof. The pews are arranged in a semicircle around the pulpit.

Originally known as the Oak Ridge Church, the congregation was formed by 13 people in 1863, making this the oldest denomination in the village. The name changed to First Congregational Church in 1871, and in 1975

First United Church of Oak Park (1917)
Holmes and Flinn, architects

75

to First United when the First Congregational Church merged with the First Presbyterian. James Scoville and the family of Ernest Hemingway were members of the congregation. The church archives record Hemingway's baptism.

Unity Temple (1905)
Frank Lloyd Wright, architect

The monolithic structure of poured, reinforced concrete
stands as the only surviving major public building
of Frank Lloyd Wright's early period.

The church complex is composed of Unity Temple
and Unity House joined by a common entrance,
courtyard and parapet. The solid mass of the facade
is crowned by square columns and the overhanging
roof. The art glass design of windows recessed
behind the columns repeats the simple geometric
ornament of the piers.

The design of the interior demonstrates Wright's
genius at transforming functional forms into art. The
interaction between receding planes and projecting
masses is almost sculptural. The oak trim unifies as it
defines the space. The skylights are composed of
simple geometric shapes.

When the congregation's church was destroyed by fire, several local architects submitted plans to design a sanctuary and meeting hall on a narrow lot within a very modest budget of $45,000. Wright, a member of the congregation, was commissioned to design the new structure.

Unity Temple is one of two National Historic Landmarks designed by Wright in the village, the other is his own home and studio at 951 Chicago Ave.

Regularly scheduled tours of the temple are available. Call (708) 848-6225 for information.

901 Lake St.

Oak Park Post Office (1933)
Charles E. White, Jr., and
Bertram Weber, architects

The main Oak Park post office is a characteristic federal government style building of the 1930s, easily recognized by its mass, classicism and formality. The stone facades are ornamented by a simple cornice, belt course and fluted entrance piers.

Metal reliefs above the entrances depict various modes of mail transport. The interior retains much of its historic integrity and includes murals painted by J. Theodore Johnson, an artist participating in the federally funded Public Works of Art Project.

The facility, completed in 1937, replaced the 1905 post office on the northeast corner of Oak Park Avenue and Lake Street. This earlier structure was sold at auction and demolished.

*Grace Episcopal Church
(1898-1922)
John Sutcliffe, architect*

This structure is a classic example of 14th-Century English Gothic Revival style architecture rendered in Indiana limestone. Flat buttresses frame the square bell tower with its crisp sculptural ornament, arched windows and crenelated parapet. The angular style of the tower relates to the steeply pitched roof and soaring gable, pierced by an elegant gothic window and stone tracery.

The interior contains an elaborately hand-carved pulpit and rood screen, bas-relief sandstone altar,and a baptistery of alabaster and marble.

Ground was broken for this structure in 1898 when the congregation outgrew a wood-frame church on Forest Avenue. Members met in the basement under a temporary flat roof while money was raised to finish the church. The structure was completed to the level of the clerestory in 1901, and the remaining building except for the tower was dedicated in 1905. The bell tower was dedicated in 1922.

The church served as a film site in 1978 for *A Wedding* and in 1990 for *Home Alone*.

Calvary Memorial Church (1901)
William G. Williamson, architect

This church was built as the First Presbyterian Church. The building was sold in 1978 to the present congregation and renamed Calvary Memorial.

This Richardsonian Romanesque building replaced an earlier frame building that had served the Presbyterian congregation for 15 years. Construction was completed in a year's time and cost about $60,000. The congregation corresponded with the building committee of Boston's renowned Trinity Church, a premier example of H. H. Richardson's architecture.

The heavy Indiana limestone arches contrast with the variegated, rough Wisconsin granite of the exterior walls. The transepts are octagonal.

Louis Millet, a designer who worked on the interiors of the Auditorium and Stock Exchange buildings, is credited with the interior design. Remnants of the original decoration are apparent in the stenciled roof timbers and balcony frieze. Historic photos show electric light bulbs in the wooden trusses of the ceiling. The narthex of the north elevation was added in 1958.

Anthony, Wilfrid Edwards

(1878-1948) of New York, was a nationally recognized architect specializing in heraldry and the design of medieval style churches. His midwestern commissions included the Dominican Priory in River Forest and the church of Notre Dame University in South Bend, Ind. [39].

Arnold, Wesley Asbury

(1850-1900) was born in Watertown, N.Y., and graduated from Syracuse University in 1879. In 1882, he was hired as a draftsman for the Chicago and North Western Railroad. After 1885, he concentrated on church architecture and designed more than 35 in the Chicago area. In 1883, Arnold married Florence Crandall, the daughter of Miles Crandall, an early Oak Park settler. In addition to his own home, Arnold designed several houses in Oak Park, including 210 S. Clinton for I. N. Conrad, 339 N. Oak Park Ave. for Ernest Hall and 300 N. Kenilworth Ave. for William J. MacDonald. He also designed the 1899 Euclid Avenue Methodist Church, which was demolished in 1922 [20].

Buck, Lawrence

(1866-1929) was born in New Orleans, La. Before opening his own practice, he was an architectural renderer working with George Maher. He was also a watercolorist, and his paintings were exhibited at the Art Institute of Chicago. In the 1880s, Buck was working in Birmingham, Ala., for the architectural firm of Sutcliffe, Armstrong and Willett. By 1894 he was in Chicago, where he again joined Sutcliffe in practice. Between 1903 and 1905 he was in Rockford, Ill. He returned to Chicago and in 1913 became a partner in the design of Cyrus H. McCormick's Lake Forest estate. Buck was not a mainstream Prairie style architect. His other Oak Park designs, such as the Edwin H. Ehrman house, 410 N. Kenilworth Ave., reflect both the influence of Frank Lloyd Wright and the Arts and Crafts movement [43].

Drummond, William

(1876-1946) was born in New Jersey, but moved to the Chicago area as a boy and grew up in Austin. The son of a carpenter, Drummond studied at the University of Illinois before joining the studio of Frank Lloyd Wright, where he rapidly rose to the status of chief draftsman. With fellow apprentice John Van Bergen, Drummond took the responsibility of completing unfinished work when Wright abandoned his Oak Park practice in 1909. Between 1912 and 1915, Drummond formed a partnership with Louis Guenzel, a draftsman in the office of Adler and Sullivan. Drummond built his own home in River Forest in 1910, as well as the United Methodist Church, 7970 Lake St. He continued to design Prairie style buildings until the 1920s, and remodeled the Rookery Building in downtown Chicago in 1931 [44].

Fiddelke, Hentry G.

(1865-1931) was born in Matteson, Illinois. During his early career he worked in the offices of Joseph L. Silsbee, Adler and Sullivan, and Jenney and Mundie. He joined Frank Ellis in Oak Park in 1894, and two years later opened his own office at 203 Marion St. He designed the Jennie A. June rowhouses, 313-319 Maple Ave., and the C. E. Hemingway House, 600 N. Kenilworth Ave. [19, 24, 25].

Frost, Charles Sumner
(1856-1931) worked for his father, a builder, before attending the Massachusetts Institute of Technology. After graduating in 1876, he worked for a number of Boston firms before joining Henry Ives Cobb in Chicago in 1882. Between 1889 and 1898, Frost practiced independently, thereafter working with Alfred Granger until 1910. Frost specialized in railway station design and was the architect for the Chicago and North Western station [68].

Granger, Alfred Hoyt
(1867-1939) was born in Zanesville, Ohio. He graduated from both the Massachusetts Institute of Technology and the Ecole des Beaux Arts in Paris. He entered the Boston office of Shepley, Rutan and Coolidge before coming to Chicago in 1891 to supervise construction on the Art Institute and the Chicago Public Library, now the Chicago Cultural Center. He practiced with Frank Meade and later Charles S. Frost before moving to Philadelphia in 1910. In 1922 he chaired the jury of the International *Chicago Tribune* Competition. In 1924 he returned to Chicago, where he worked until retiring to Connecticut in 1936. He was a captain in the United States Engineering Corps and chairman of the War Industries Board's construction committee [68].

Holmes, Morris Grant
(1862-1945) was born in Laporte, Ind. His architectural career began in 1882 with the Chicago office of Solon S. Beman. In 1895 he moved to Buffalo, N.Y., but returned to Chicago in 1912 to join Patton and Flinn, which became Holmes and Flinn after 1915. He worked on the design of the Oak Park Club, 721 Ontario St., West Suburban Hospital, 518 N. Austin Blvd., and buildings in Fenchow, China. Holmes practiced in Chicago for 50 years and resided in Hyde Park [75].

Holsman, Henry K.
(1866 -1960) was the chief designer in a partnership with W. L. Brainer that lasted from 1893 to 1897. In 1900 he designed and patented the "Holsman" automobile, the first two-cylinder car in this country. He designed a number of apartment houses in the Hyde Park and Kenwood areas of Chicago, and was a partner in the real estate firm of Parker and Holsman [65].

Hotchkiss, Roy J.
(1877-1945) was born in Richmond, Ind., and moved to Oak Park at the age of seven. Hotchkiss was an apprentice in E. E. Roberts' Oak Park studio before opening his own office at 115 N. Oak Park Ave. In addition to his design of the Medical Arts Building, he designed the 1920 commercial structure at 720 Lake St., the 1941 Church of the Good Shepherd, 611 Randolph St., as well as churches in Elmhurst and Morris, Ill., and several houses in Oak Park [71, 72, 73].

Maher, George Washington
(1864-1926) was born in Mill Creek, W. Va. His family moved to Chicago where their dreams of prosperity were never fulfilled. Maher was an apprentice in the architectural office of Bauer and Hill at the age of 18. In the early 1880s he moved to the office of Joseph L. Silsbee, where he obtained the greater part of his architectural training and met Frank Lloyd Wright. In 1888 Maher launched his own practice designing many homes in Edgewater and Kenilworth, communities he also helped plan. Maher, like Louis Sullivan and John Root, advocated the rejection of traditional styles and a search for a new and indigenous American style. He designed several homes on Chicago's North Shore, as well as buildings at Northwestern University [8].

McCarthy, Joseph William
(1884-1965) was born in Jersey City,
N.J. He attended school in New York
and Chicago before joining the firm of
D. H. Burnham and Company as an
apprentice draftsman. McCarthy
established his own practice in 1910,
but during World War I joined Graham,
Anderson, Probst and White, former
partners at Burnham and Company.
McCarthy was a friend and "court
architect" to George Cardinal
Mundelein. Among his church-related
commissions, were three cathedrals,
four hospitals, Mundelein Seminary,
and forty-three churches, including St.
Catherines, St. Giles and St. Lukes in
the area [60].

Pashley, Alfred F.
(1856-1932) was born in Arlington
County, Wisc. He attended school in
Chicago and classes at the Art Institute.
His architectural training was acquired
under private instructors and in Europe.
He established a partnership with James
H. Willett around 1880. Together they
are credited with innovative hospital
planning, the 1880 design of the
Chicago archbishop's residence, 1555
N. State Parkway, and the 1893 reno-
vation of Holy Name Cathedral [18].

Patton, Normand Smith
(1852-1915) was born in Hartford,
Conn., educated at Amherst and graduated from the Massachusetts Institute of
Technology in 1874. He opened an
office in Chicago and after 1878
formed several successive partnerships.
He was an architect for government
agencies in Washington, D.C., and
Chicago. In Oak Park he designed the
1885 Scoville Institute and joined
Robert Spencer in the design of the
1905 high school building. His Chicago
designs include, the 1893 Chicago
Academy of Sciences, buildings for the
Armour Institute, which now house the
Illinois Institute of Technology, and

several Chicago churches. He resided
at 225 N. Grove Ave. in Oak Park [7,
70, 72, 73].

Roberts, Eben Ezra
(1866-1943) was born in Boston and
learned mechanical and freehand drawing from his father. After attending
Tilton Academy in New Hampshire, in
1889 he was hired by the Chicago firm
S. S. Beman as clerk of the works. In
1893, he opened his own office in Oak
Park, which became the largest architectural practice in the village.
Advertising himself as an architect of
"homey dwellings," he specialized in
residential design and stucco. In July
1911, *Cement Era* recognized Roberts'
"particular study" of stucco and his
"determination of working out an architectural design especially adopted to
it." *Rock Products*, another trade publi-
cation of the same date, saluted Roberts
as "the first architect in Chicago to give
cement its proper recognition in residence architecture." The architect's Oak
Park home and studio were at 1019
Superior St. [5, 13, 14, 32, 34, 40,
41, 42, 46, 64, 72, 74].

Schlacks, Henry John
(1868-1938) was born in Chicago and
trained as a draftsman in the offices of
Adler and Sullivan. After two years of
study at the Massachusetts Institute of
Technology, he traveled extensively in
Europe. The sketches he made on tour
later served as the basis for many of his
designs. After returning to Chicago, he
became a partner of Henry Ottenheimer
and later opened his own practice
concentrating on the design of Catholic
churches. Among his Chicago designs
are: St. Martin's, St. Paul's, St. Boniface,
St. Adelbert and St. John of God.
[27, 28].

Schock, Frederick R.
(1854-1934) was born in Chicago and
began his architectural career at the

age of 18 with Henry L. Gay. In 1880 he joined S. S. Beman, where he worked on the design of Pullman. He established his own practice in Chicago and moved to Austin. The houses he designed in Douglas Park, Garfield Park, Kenwood and Oak Park are mainly Queen Anne, Shingle or modified Prairie style structures [69].

Sutcliffe, John
(1853-1913) was born in Lancashire, England. He worked as a naval architect for the British government but returned home to continue an architectural practice established by his father. In 1886, he moved to New York and on to Boston and Birmingham, Ala. He established a partnership with Armstrong and Willett, where he met Lawrence Buck. In 1892 he moved to Chicago, became a city building inspector, and worked for Henry Ives Cobb designing buildings for the University of Chicago. In 1893 he formed a short-lived architectural practice with Buck, and began to concentrate on designing Gothic Revival churches. Sutcliffe, who designed some 100 churches, lived in Oak Park and was an authority on Gothic architecture [78].

Van Bergen, John S.
(1885-1969) was a native of Oak Park and neighbor of Walter Burley Griffin, an architect who left the studio of Frank Lloyd Wright around 1906. Van Bergen was a draftsman in Griffin's office for two years before enrolling in architectural classes at the Chicago Technical College. In 1909, he became the last person hired in Wright's Oak Park studio, supervising unfinished projects after Wright left for Europe. In 1910 he was hired by William Drummond, another former Wright apprentice. The following year Van Bergen established his own practice. His Prairie style houses are known for their careful planning

and simplicity. He moved to Ravinia after World War I and to Santa Barbara, Calif., in 1955 [26, 49, 51].

Van Keuren, William J.
(1853-1915), a native of Cincinnati, moved to Chicago as a young man. He resided in Oak Park for 30 years and maintained offices at 84 La Salle St. in Chicago. He built numerous Stick and Queen Anne style homes in Chicago, Oak Park, River Forest, Maywood and Austin. His designs include: the S. A. Rothermel rowhouses, 100-110 S. Home Ave.; the Emerson Ingalls rowhouses, 200-208 Forest Avenue; the William H. Cribben house, 330 S. Euclid Ave.; as well as the 1899 village fire station at Lombard Avenue and Lake Street., which has been converted for use by the local water department [3, 4].

White, Charles Elmer, Jr.,
(1876-1936) was born in Boston and studied at the Massachusetts Institute of Technology. In 1895 he became an industrial designer for Swift Brothers Meat Packers. He worked for the American Gas Company in Philadelphia and street railway companies in Ohio and Indiana before entering Frank Lloyd Wright's Oak Park studio in 1903. Two years later, he established his own firm, and between 1923 and 1932 was a partner with Bertram Weber. He was the first chairman of the village's zoning board. Late in his career, White participated in several slum clearance projects on Chicago's north side. He contributed articles to *House Beautiful*, the *Ladies Home Journal* and *Country Life in America*. He also published *Successful Homes and How to Build Them* and *The Bungalow Book* [2, 12, 77].

Willett, James Howland
(1831-1907) was born in Dublin, Ireland, but moved to Philadelphia as a child. He studied architecture and

moved to Chicago after the Civil War. He opened an office in 1876 and the following year built the first large apartment house in the city. He joined Alfred Pashley in practice around 1880. Together they were involved in hospital planning and designed several projects for the Chicago Archdiocese [18].

Wright, Frank Lloyd
(1867-1959) was born in Richland Center, Wisc., and spent one year at the University of Wisconsin before moving to Chicago in 1887. He trained with Joseph Lyman Silsbee and moved to the offices of Adler and Sullivan, where he worked from 1888 to 1893. He established an independent practice first in the city of Chicago and then in Oak Park. His early Queen Anne and Shingle style work evolved during his Oak Park years into simple, bold, geometric buildings, whose horizontal character and broad roofs earned the title "Prairie style." While in Oak Park, Wright designed more than 125 buildings and trained more than 20 apprentices in his studio. In 1909 Wright left for Europe, where he published a large and influential drawing portfolio. In 1911 he closed his Oak Park studio, returned to Wisconsin to build Taliesin and established an architectural fellowship in Spring Green. He later built a third home and studio near Phoenix, Ariz. Wright's impact on Oak Park elevated the village from a center of provincial architecture to one of international acclaim [11, 76].

Barclay, Philander. Oak Park as Seen by Philander Barclay. Oak Park, Ill.: Historical Society of Oak Park and River Forest, 1976.

Block, Jean F. Hyde Park Houses: An Informal History, 1856-1910. Chicago, Ill.: The University of Chicago Press, 1978.

Bluestone, Daniel. Guide to the Architecture in the Ridgeland-Oak Park Historic District. Oak Park, Ill.: Oak Park Landmarks Commission, 1983.

Brooke, Lee. Oak Park's Avenue Lake Plaza. Oak Park, Ill., 1984.

Brooke, Lee. Yesterday When I Was Younger. Oak Park, Ill., 1989.

Butters, George. "Early Ridgeland." Oak Park, Ill.

Chicago, Illinois. Archdiocese of Chicago. Archives.

Cook, May Estelle. Little Old Oak Park. Oak Park, Ill., 1961.

Directory of Oak Park, Illinois. Oak Park, Ill., 1901, 1903, 1905, and 1912.

Frank Lloyd Wright Home and Studio Foundation. Volunteer Training Manual. Oak Park, Ill.: Frank Lloyd Wright Home and Studio Foundation, 1992.

Guarino, Jean. Oak Park: A Pictorial History. St. Louis: G. Bradley Publishing, Inc., 1988.

Halley, William. Pictorial Oak Park. Oak Park, Ill., 1898.

Hasbrouck, Wilbert R., and Sprague, Paul E. A Survey of Historic Architecture of the Village of Oak Park, Illinois. 2nd ed., Oak Park Historic Preservation Commission. Oak Park, Ill.: Village of Oak Park, 1992.

Hoagland, Gertrude Fox. Historical Survey of Oak Park, Illinois. Oak Park, Ill.: Oak Park Public Library, 1937.

Le Gacy, Arthur Evans. Improvers and Preservers: A History of Oak Park, Illinois, 1823-1940. Chicago, Ill., 1967.

Oak Leaves, April 22, 1905.

Oak Leaves, May 27, 1905.

Oak Leaves, April 27, 1907.

Oak Leaves, Oct. 16, 1907.

Oak Leaves, Sept. 28, 1912.

Oak Leaves, March 18, 1916.

Oak Leaves, July 12, 1978.

Oak Leaves, July 27, 1983.

Oak Park, Illinois. Euclid Avenue United Methodist Church. Archives.

Oak Park, Illinois. First Congregational Church of Oak Park. Archives.

Oak Park, Illinois. First Presbyterian Church. Archives.

Oak Park, Illinois. First United Church of Oak Park. Archives.

Oak Park, Illinois. Frank Lloyd Wright Home and Studio

Foundation Research Center. Building permit files.

Oak Park, Illinois. Grace Episcopal Church. Archives.

Oak Park, Illinois. Historical Society of Oak Park and River Forest. Building files.

Oak Park, Illinois. Oak Park Public Library. Local history files.

Oak Park, Illinois. Oak Park Village Hall. Building permit files.

Oak Park, Illinois. St. Edmund Church. Archives.

River Forest Herald, Sept. 9, 1892.

Sanborn Fire Insurance Map Company. Map of Chicago, Illinois, Cook County, Sections of Oak Park, Ridgeland and Austin. Vol. C, 1895.

Sprague, Paul E. Guide to Frank Lloyd Wright and Prairie School Architecture in Oak Park. 5th ed., Oak Park Landmarks Commission. Oak Park, Ill.: Village of Oak Park, 1986.

Steiner, Frances H. Victorian Oak Park: Five Architectural Tours. Chicago, Ill.: Sigma Press, 1983.

Stilgoe, John R. Borderland: Origins of the American Suburb 1820-1939. New Haven, Conn.: Yale University Press, 1988.

Village of Oak Park. Oak Park Comprehensive Plan, 1973-1992. Oak Park, Ill., 1972.

Withey, Henry F. and Withey, Elsie Rathburn. Biographical Dictionary of American Architects, Deceased. Los Angeles: Hennessey and Ingalls, 1970.

Photo Credits

Ridgeland-Oak Park Historic District

1 121 S. Maple Ave.
2 1139 Randolph St.
3 329 S. Wisconsin Ave.
4 1101 South Blvd.
5 1111 South Blvd.
6 112-114 S. Home Ave.
7 210 S. Home Ave.
8 217 S. Home Ave.
9 241 S. Home Ave.
10 304 S. Home Ave.
11 404 S. Home Ave.
12 420 S. Clinton Ave.
13 412 S. Clinton Ave.
14 321 S. Clinton Ave.
15 308 S. Clinton Ave.
16 305 S. Clinton Ave.
17 211 S. Clinton Ave
18 200-208 S. Clinton Ave.
19 138 S. Clinton Ave.
20 130 S. Kenilworth Ave.

21 247-249 S. Kenilworth Ave.
22 235 S. Grove Ave.
23 213 S. Grove Ave.
24 209 S. Grove Ave.
25 139 S. Grove Ave.
26 106 S. Grove Ave.
27 188 S. Oak Park Ave.
28 208 S. Oak Park Ave.
29 815-821 W. Washington Blvd.
30 408 S. Oak Park Ave.
31 711-713 W. Washington Blvd.
32 405 S. Euclid Ave.
33 661 W. Washington Blvd.
34 324 S. Euclid Ave.
35 214 S. Euclid Ave.
36 201 S. Wesley Ave.
37 229 S. Wesley Ave.
38 626 W. Washington Blvd.
39 505 W. Washington Blvd.
40 108 -118 S. East Ave.

41 213-215 S. Elmwood Ave.
42 241 S. Elmwood Ave.
43 300 S. Elmwood Ave.
44 410 W. Washington Blvd.
45 321, 325, 328 S. Ridgeland Ave.
46 224 S. Ridgeland Ave.
47 115 S. Ridgeland Ave.
48 103 -113 S. Ridgeland Ave.
   101 -111 South Blvd.
49 202 S. Cuyler Ave.
50 237-241 W. Washington Blvd.
51 418 S. Harvey Ave.
52 127-133 S. Harvey Ave.
53 134 -140 S. Harvey Ave.
   220 -226 Pleasant St.
54 117 S. Lombard Ave.
55 206-210 S. Lombard Ave.
   119-127 Pleasant St.
56 301 S. Lombard Ave.
57 202 W. Washington Blvd.
58 415-427 S. Taylor Ave.

59 430 S. Taylor Ave.
60 38 N. Austin Blvd.
61 324 S. Humphrey Ave.
62 146-154 N. Humphrey Ave.
63 412 N. Austin Blvd.
64 518 N. Austin Blvd.
65 301 N. Taylor Ave.
66 300 Block N. Taylor Ave.
67 144 N. Cuyler Ave.
68 171 N. Cuyler Ave.
69 400-404 Lake St.
   135-141 N. Ridgeland Ave.
70 460 Lake St.
71 715 Lake St.
72 116-136 N. Oak Park Ave.
73 115 N. Oak Park Ave.
74 129-151 N. Oak Park Ave.
75 848 Lake St.
76 875 Lake St.
77 901 Lake St.
78 924 Lake St.
79 931 Lake St.